Achievement
in non-accredited learning
for adults with
learning difficulties

Report of the scoping study

Liz Maudslay and
Christine Nightingale

niace

promoting adult learning

department for
education and skills
creating opportunity, releasing potential, achieving excellence

Acknowledgements

With many thanks to all the learning providers who responded to the NIACE questionnaire and to those who told us about their experiences and practices.

Thank you also to Dr Lesley Dee for her expertise and advice and to the members of the RARPA steering group for sharing knowledge.

©2004 National Institute of Adult Continuing Education
(England and Wales)

21 De Montfort Street
Leicester
LE1 7GE

Company registration no. 2603322
Charity registration no. 1002775

NIACE has a broad remit to promote lifelong learning opportunities for adults. NIACE works to develop increased participation in education and training, particularly for those who do not have easy access because of class, gender, age, race, language and culture, learning difficulties or disabilities, or insufficient financial resources.

You can find NIACE online at **www.niace.org.uk**

Cataloguing in Publication Data
A CIP record of this title is available from the British Library

Designed and typeset by Boldface
Print and bound in the UK by Latimer Trend
ISBN: 1 86201 211 3

Contents

Introduction

Currently there is a great deal of emphasis on identifying and recording the achievement of learners following accredited learning provision. However, there has been less emphasis on recognising and recording how learners make progress in areas which are not accredited, either when they are on non-accredited learning programmes, or when they make progress when on an accredited programme but in areas which are not themselves formally accredited.

As this report was being researched and written, the Learning and Skills Council was funding development projects led by the National Institute of Adult Continuing Education and the Learning and Skills Development Agency on 'Recognising and Recording Progress and Achievement (RARPA) in Non-accredited Learning'.

The RARPA programme projects involved a range of different learning-providers, two of which are specialist colleges for adults with learning difficulties. However, the other sites did not focus specifically on the needs and experiences of this particular learner group. The majority of adults with learning difficulties in post-compulsory education are attending further education colleges either on specialist programmes or in ordinary classes. Because of their learning difficulties learners in this cohort are very likely to be attending provision which is not formally accredited. When they are attending accredited learning programmes they may also have additional learning goals which may not be externally accredited but still need to be recognised and assessed. It is the needs of these learners that this report investigates.

The brief

NIACE was contracted by the Department for Education and Skills to identify issues for providers and learners in recognising and recording progress and achievement for learners with learning difficulties. Importantly, we wanted to identify current thinking, knowledge and practice both by reviewing relevant literature and by carrying out a survey of providers and practitioners.

The objectives of the project were to:

- carry out a literature survey of work which informs current thinking on recognising and recording achievement in non-accredited learning with adults with learning difficulties;

- identify, collect and analyse evidence to illustrate current practice from across the post-16 education spectrum;

- disseminate the evidence and findings of the project to policy-makers and practitioners; and

- contribute findings to the larger RARPA programme

RARPA

The Recognising and Recording Progress and Achievement project (a joint LSC, NIACE and LSDA venture) is facilitating a range of learning-provider sites to develop and test out a process for capturing learner achievement in non-accredited programmes (LSC, 2003).

Using a five-stage model devised after consultation with the inspectorate and consistent with the common inspection framework, sites create or build on existing systems for recognising learner progress. The five stages are:

1. Setting the aim of the programme of learning which may define its general purpose, or may be more specific (curriculum design).

2. Initial assessment of the learner, to find out what the learner's needs and aspirations are. This is an important stage in the process, as it enables learners to express their desires, interests, motivations and support needs. It can, if undertaken during induction, promote a greater understanding of the purpose of the programme and enable learners and teachers to get to know each other. Importantly, in the process of recording progression, it can establish where the starting-point is for that learner and identify what they want to achieve by undertaking the learning.

3. Identification of learning objectives which meet the stated planned learning outcomes of the programme of learning for the learner group and the individual learner.

4. Formative assessment, or the ways in which teachers identify and record progress made by the learners. This may be a very creative process with suggestions of video recordings, learner diaries, exhibitions as well as more traditional assignments and tests.

5. End of programme review of progress and achievement, which may involve learner or peer-group assessment, teacher's record of assessment, and a whole range of artefacts as appropriate to the programme of study (summative assessment).

Area of study

Most of the attention in provision for people with learning difficulties is on non-accredited programmes. That is, programmes which do not attract external accreditation but could attract an internal certificate. The focus of this study is on adults with learning difficulties in both discrete and integrated provision who are not following accredited programmes.

As a scoping study, we took a two-pronged approach to identifying the issues. As both approaches were simultaneous, our learning from each naturally influenced our approach to the other. The juxtaposition and comparison of both types of data enabled issues and themes to be triangulated, refined and new and further issues identified. For example if an adult learning provider mentioned a specific model for identifying learners' needs we would then ensure that we looked for this in our review of the literature.

Method 1: literature review

Essentially this was where the scoping study began. A wide-ranging search of current and reported research across social sciences, education, health and social care was undertaken to identify key issues and themes for this report. Education, health and social care databases were searched and references were sought from other expert researchers in the fields. We were keen to identify issues from other sectors whose work with adults with learning difficulties could impact on the learning processes.

Method 2: a survey of post-16 providers

We surveyed a range of provision, including further education, adult and community learning, Entry to Employment (E2E), work-based learning and sixth form colleges, who were not known to be engaged in the RARPA development projects. Around 200 questionnaires were posted out and a copy of the questionnaire was posted on the NIACE website.

The aim of this survey was to draw out current practice among providers not involved in the RARPA projects and to test some of the themes emerging from the literature. The scoping study was designed to complement and contribute to the RARPA projects. The questionnaire was designed to enable qualitative responses to questions.

We recognised that there is a wide range of practice in the field, so it was important to capture this in written responses to fairly open questions rather than constrain responders to a limited or narrow range of responses. Eighty-seven completed questionnaires were received (see Table 1); these were generally completed by managers responsible for the curriculum for learners with learning difficulties. Ten of the sites were then followed up with a visit or telephone interview to pursue their responses more intensely. The visits included discussions with curriculum managers, classroom teachers and in one case a classroom observation and feedback from learners.

Adults with learning difficulties

It is our belief that finding ways of evaluating and measuring non-accredited learning is particularly important for people with learning difficulties. These learners have often found it very hard to attain recognised, external measures of achievement and may see themselves as failing, in terms of usually recognised benchmarks of achievement. They may also have very individual styles of learning which have never been fully explored and recognised. In addition they may have uneven levels of achievement, or 'spiky profiles', which mean they can achieve in certain areas while having some difficulties in others. Finally, there is a necessity for formative assessment, a strong connection between assessment and the learning people do, and hence a vital link between formative and summative assessment.

Each of the steps listed in the RARPA five-stage model (described above, p 7) is extremely important for learners with learning difficulties. However, there are ways in which these learners may require additional approaches if they are to be genuinely of benefit to them:

- **Initial assessment** may take considerably longer with these learners, who might find it hard to conceptualise and articulate their aspirations and own learning goals. Indeed, assessment needs to be seen not as a one-off initial event but as part of an ongoing process throughout the learning programme.

- Many adults with learning difficulties are receiving support from a range of service providers. If a learner's educational programme is to form part of a holistic plan it may be important for education staff, with the learner's consent, to **collaborate with staff from other agencies** and people close to the learner.

- Helping learners to identify **specific learning objectives** which will contribute to their own aspirations may take longer and need to be worked through in more detail.

- The **steps** which constitute progress may be very small, require close observation, and not be measurable against standardised outcomes.

- The process of **formative assessment** is very important for all learners. Observing exactly how learners learn best, what they can do well and how to build this into the next stage of their programme is vitally important.

- Learners may have very different levels of skills in different areas and **existing attainment must be recognised** appropriately. (An interesting example of this was recorded by an inspector who was observing an 'independent living skills' class for learners with learning difficulties in which the learners were learning how to iron. One learner had great ability in this area: it transpired that he had a role in his family whereby he did all the ironing. However, in the class he was being treated along with all the others as being a complete beginner.)

- Having learning outcomes recognised formally can be very important for these learners who have often had no formal recognition of their learning. **Affirming success**, for example in the form of college certificates, can form a part of their assessment.

When dealing with adults with learning difficulties there is a particular danger of imposing ideas of what others *think* learners need, rather than really listening to what they are saying. This can be particularly true in the area of 'independent living skills', where programmes are created based on the curriculum writers' view of what constitutes 'skills for independence', which may not be completely in line with what the learners themselves need. The warning note mentioned by Grief and Windsor (2003) is particularly relevant here. It is very important that, when defining what needs to be evaluated, one does not end up creating a rigid checklist, which in turn denies the essential flexibility needed to design programmes.

The legislative context

The *Disability Discrimination Act* (1995) was the first piece of UK legislation to give specific rights to disabled people. Education came under this Act in 2001 (*Disability Discrimination Act Part 4*, 2001). DDA Part 4 states the need for post-school education providers 'not to discriminate against disabled students for a reason related to their disability' and to provide disabled students with 'reasonable adjustments' . The nature of these duties is spelled out in the Code of Practice which accompanies the Act (Disability Rights Commission, 2002).

The implementation of DDA Part 4 has led to the production of literature and guidance for those working in post-school education (Association of Colleges, 2002; DfES Guidance, 2002a; NIACE, 2003 (*New Rights to Learn*)). These publications do not deal specifically with issues of recognising and recording learner progression and achievement in non-accredited learning. They do, however, remind the provider of the need to make 'reasonable adjustments' for adults with learning difficulties. One important way in which these 'reasonable adjustments' can be made is through finding ways of listening to learners' aspirations when undertaking a learning programme.

Review of the literature and survey findings

Literature from education, health and social care and disability sources was reviewed. The aim was to identify issues that helped to clarify the needs and perspectives of learners, learning-providers, teachers, policy-makers, health workers, staff in social care and family carers.

The review of the literature was intended both to report on the current position of recognising and recording achievement and to identify key themes that impact on the whole process. For example, we were keen to explore the concepts and practice of partnership and collaborative working with other agencies and other approaches to assessment and need identification. In particular we explored the processes of person-centred planning as articulated in the White Paper *Valuing People* (DoH, 2000).

As the focus is on adults we have not looked in depth at literature related to learning in schools. There are, however, some references to approaches adopted in schools for dealing with learners with learning difficulties where they help to illuminate post-school methods.

The review will begin by examining the work carried out by Grief and Windsor (2003) on recognising and validating achievement in non-accredited work in literacy, language and numeracy. It will then examine a range of current literature in tandem with a summary of the survey findings, grouping works and survey findings under the headings of the five stages of the RARPA approach.

Why is it important to recognise achievement and progression?

Both the LSC (2003) and Grief and Windsor (2003) identify why there is a need for non-accredited provision to be available for certain learners. They suggest that provision without accreditation:

- offers the chance to build confidence, particularly for those who may have previous poor learning experiences;

- provides opportunities to negotiate individual learning plans;

- can create success by breaking learning into small 'bite-sized chunks';

- enables appropriate goals to be set, particularly for those learners who progress slowly and for whom gaining a qualification is a long way off;

- responds to learners who have 'spiky profiles' (that is, they may have better skills or knowledge in parts of the subject they are learning than in others);

- offers an environment which avoids learning opportunities for learners who cannot demonstrate required skills because of a learning difficulty or disability;

- is often embedded into other courses (it may not be possible to accredit these elements within such courses).

Potential problems with this approach

Grief and Windsor (2003) identified problems with recognising achievement. Many of these stem, of course, from poor definitions of original objectives. Learners who may be lacking in self-esteem or confidence may be their own harshest critics. So if an objective is written in a way that is not SMART (specific, measurable, achievable, realistic and time-bound) learners and teachers might find it difficult to recognise that any progress or achievement has been made.

Some educational establishments have attempted to find ways of measuring learners' success according to individual outcomes. For example, Baxter (2001) records how in Colchester they devised a system which recorded the proportion of learners who achieved a benchmark percentage of their intended learning outcomes. At the time of writing they were about to evaluate a procedure whereby a pass is awarded when learners achieve 70 per cent or more of the intended learning outcomes.

Whilst it is tempting to try to quantify how much progression and achievement a learner has made, the LSC suggest (LSC, 2003) that most providers find that the data is not robust enough to stand up to comparative analysis. The LSC (2003) report also states that some providers are concerned that the assessment can become an end in itself and create a situation where end-of-programme assessment takes on greater importance than ongoing formative approaches; hence providers become more concerned with learner outcomes than with overall learner development. Grief and Windsor (2003), too, give a word of warning of the danger that, in attempting to measure non-accredited learning, one can actually lose the freedom and individuality of a non-accredited programme. This can be particularly true in work with learners with learning difficulties (Sutcliffe and Jacobsen, 1998; FEFC, 1999) and this issue is returned to in some of the work which follows.

In presenting the literature review and results of our survey we have attempted to situate works and evidence within the five stages of the RARPA model. However, the texts and data we refer to do not necessarily fit neatly into these categories, hence there is inevitable overlap between sections.

1 Curriculum design

The first step of the RARPA 'staged process' talks about the need to explore the aims of the learning programme. Learners with learning difficulties might be attending a range of learning programmes: they might be on a college course specifically designed for learners with learning difficulties, they might be attending other college or adult education courses (either part time or full time), or they might be taking part in an Entry to Employment programme.

Types of provision

Of the 87 respondents to our questionnaire, 17 claimed to have only discrete or segregated learning provision for adults with learning difficulties, sixty providers made both ordinary and discrete courses available and nine had only ordinary provision.

Table 1. Types of provision for adults with learning difficulties

Provider type	No responses	Discrete provision only	Ordinary provision only	Mixed opportunities	Totals
Sixth form college	1	1	8	5	15
Voluntary sector		1	1	2	4
LEA/work-based learning		1		1	2
Specialist college for learners with learning difficulties		1			1
LEA		1		9	10
Further education college		12		39	51
Work-based learning				1	1
WEA				1	1
Mixed				2	2
Totals	**1**	**17**	**9**	**60**	**87**

In order to try to understand the different models of curriculum design for specialist provision for post-school learners with learning difficulties, one needs to take a historical view of the kind of curricula which have been used. During the 1980s and 1990s many colleges responded to the needs of learners with learning difficulties by creating discrete curricula based on 'independence and life skills'. While theoretically allowing space for the development of a learner-centred curriculum based on individual aspirations, there are ways in which such courses can develop into a specific view of what constitutes independence that may be at odds with the views of individuals on this course. As early as 1989 Jenny Corbett spoke of how forcing learners into staff expectations of what constituted independence could become 'another form of oppression' (Corbett, 1989, p 159). In particular, if learners are from a minority ethnic group they may have slightly different views of what independence means – views which may be at odds with staff expectations (Skill, 2003)

In 1996 the FEFC established a committee to look at inclusive learning in further education; its report (FEFC, 1996) strongly emphasised the need for colleges to respond to individual learner requirements and address individual learning styles. Influential as this report was, it could at times be seen as being at odds with the funding methodology which emphasised 'consumerism, performance and efficiency' (Dee, 1999). During the 1990s a desire to provide a formally accredited outcome to learners with learning difficulties resulted in a huge expansion in the number of national awards for students with learning difficulties. However, concern was expressed that the pressure to follow externally validated awards was leading some practitioners to use the award as a substitute for planning curricula based on individual priorities (FEFC, 1999).

In the years immediately following the establishment of the Learning and Skills Council in 2000 the dominant pressure felt by teachers of adults with learning difficulties appears to be the perceived need to be following a 'basic skills' curriculum. Several teachers feel they have been pressurised into this curriculum area by their managers and this can result in learners following an inappropriate and narrow curriculum based on a limited and outcome-based notion of literacy, language and numeracy.

In each of the instances mentioned above, curriculum design becomes teacher-led and based on what the learner cannot do, rather than looking at learner potential, learner aspiration and the interaction of the learner with their environment (Cline, 1992). Interestingly, this choice of curriculum came about through perceived rather than actual direction from above. The FEFC did not, in fact, require courses for learners with learning difficulties to be accredited, while the LSC does not insist on these learners adhering to a basic skills programme. However, in both cases, the prevailing culture, which was heavily biased in a particular direction, translated itself into practice in the area of learning difficulties. It is important now to examine the moves there have been to move learning-difficulty work towards a more learner-focused perspective.

In the schools sector, since the advent of the National Curriculum, there has been considerable work on how to secure individualised curricula within a shared national curriculum (Ouvry and Saunders, 2001; QCA/DfES, 2001). In post-school education there have been two recent national guidance documents for those working with adults with learning difficulties at entry or at pre-entry level. The first was the *Adult Pre-Entry Curriculum Framework for Literacy and Numeracy* (DfES, 2002b), which looks specifically at the areas of communication and numeracy and shows how these do not need to be narrowly interpreted but can be used creatively to address the particular communication needs of individuals. It particularly focuses on the areas of non-written, and at times non-verbal, communication and also emphasises the importance of moving learning outside the confines of the classroom.

The second is the *QCA Guidance for Post-school Learners* (QCA, 2002). This guidance focuses in some detail on how to plan a learner-centred curriculum for young adults operating mainly or entirely below Level 1. This guidance is not about designing a new curriculum but about looking at how staff can create a learner-centred approach within an existing curriculum. It is organised around four key sections:

1. Values, which must underpin all planning to ensure that adults with learning difficulties can participate in society as active citizens with associated rights.

2. Planning, which includes:
   - exploring and developing individual aspirations;
   - how to use this knowledge in planning an individual learning programme;
   - how to discover how this learner learns best and what strategies would best support him or her;
   - what resources are needed and how to make best use of them; and
   - monitoring success, recognising achievement and moving on.

3. Evaluation, which gives staff a framework in which to ensure that they really are responding to learner needs.

4. A series of 30 case studies showing how individual learners with learning difficulties have been helped to follow through a programme of study which supports their individual wishes and aspirations.

The case studies make clear that this guidance is not just for staff working on courses specifically designed for learners with learning difficulties, but for staff teaching on any courses which might include these learners – for instance it gives an example of a young woman who wishes to move from stacking shelves in a supermarket to working on the till and has very clear outcomes that she wishes to achieve from attending a college numeracy learning programme.

In the next section on initial assessment we will explore further this polarity between teacher-led and learner-led perspectives. However, first it is important to look at other curricula which adults with learning difficulties might be following. As we will show, many of the respondents to our questionnaire believed that the process of identifying learners' hopes and aspirations has encouraged a more focused curriculum and influenced programme design.

Entry to Employment (E2E)

Many people with learning difficulties are clear that employment, whether part-time or full-time, is an important outcome for them. Currently, access to work-based learning programmes for people with learning difficulties is variable. It is to be hoped that with the LSC's wider remit, which includes work-based learning, and with the development of Entry to Employment, there will be a more consistent representation of people with learning difficulties in work-based learning provision.

Entry to Employment is designed to accommodate all young learners working below Level 2. The *Framework for Entry to Employment Programmes* (LSC, 2002) gives a refreshing description of a work-based learning programme unconstricted by an adherence to external validation. It emphasises the importance of creating flexible, individual programmes that put the young person at their centre by 'meeting individual need' and 'taking account of young people's views'. When speaking of attainment it states that (LSC, 2002, para.6.2) while external qualifications may, where appropriate, form a part of the programme, the RARPA process whereby progress is judged against learner objectives 'is deeply embedded throughout E2E programmes'.

In an E2E Accreditation Forum in March 2003 there was discussion about the main learning points and actions from the E2E Accreditation Conference. Sadly, despite the strong emphasis on non-accredited learning in the *Framework* there was still a feeling that 'there was a danger of death by accreditation in E2E'. The paper reveals the inherent tension between, on the one hand, learners' own desire for formal validation and, on the other hand, the recognition that external accreditation can force learners into learning which does not best meet their own particular learning needs. This is likely to be particularly true for learners on E2E who have learning difficulties, and exemplifies the need both to improve the quality and raise the status of non-accredited learning. The Accreditation Forum also looked at how progress in non-accredited areas might best be presented in a way which helped employers to recognise skills which had been gained, and the DfES Progress File was highlighted as a good way of doing this.

Also in the work-based learning area, a DfES report *Measuring Soft Outcomes and Distance Travelled: A Review of Current Practice*, (Dewson *et al.*, 2000) has evaluated certain ESF programmes dealing with people disadvantaged in the labour market to see how far they managed to measure and record the 'soft outcomes' and 'distance travelled' of learners on the programmes. They recognise that these outcomes may need to be 'group-specific' and give the example of projects catering for learners with mental health difficulties or learning difficulties, where outcomes could include 'a greater level of self-awareness, or lowered anxiety'. While recognising the danger of subjectivity in such measurement, the authors conclude that such outcomes are essential, both to learners and to potential employers, and staff need to find more effective ways of identifying and recording them.

2 Initial assessment/ listening to learners

The second stage in the RARPA process talks about the need to listen to learners and find out what their needs and aspirations are.

In the early days of special schools, theories of teaching tended to be teacher-led, with staff assessing students' needs and setting precise, observable, measurable and behaviourally quantifiable objectives for each learner. Babbage, Byers and Redding (1999) trace the challenges to this method and the move to a more experiential and constructionist approach underpinned by principles of:

- making a wide variety of interesting materials and resources freely accessible and available to learners;

- encouraging pupils to handle and explore materials at will;

- encouraging pupils to choose preferred activities and select their own materials and resources;

- valuing all the communicative attempts made by learners; and

- using adults as supporters…allowing the pupil to take the initiative.

James (1998) writes of how 'constructivists…argue that an assessment system intended to improve the quality of learning should not treat students as imperfect learners, but as people who are actively trying to make sense of what they are taught'. Cline (1992, chapter 8) looks at four models of assessment of children with special needs:

- assessment focusing on the child and his/her disability;

- assessment focusing on the teaching programme and attempts to match this very closely to the child's existing skills and knowledge;

- assessment focused on the zone of potential development; and

- assessment focused on the learning environment.

He shows how the first two of these types of assessment, where the role of the pupil is passive, can – on their own – create a deficit and narrow model of learning. He emphasises the importance of looking both at emerging skills and understanding and at the interaction between the child and the learning environment. Lunt (in Daniels, 1992) compares 'static' versus 'dynamic' assessment, showing how static assessment focuses on the product rather than the process of learning while dynamic assessment procedures involve 'a dynamic interactional exploration of a learner's learning and thinking processes'.

This interactive approach to assessment, whereby the autonomy of people with learning difficulties is respected and they are listened to, forms the basis of the self-advocacy movement of people with learning difficulties. Over the past 15–20 years strong self-advocacy movements for people with learning difficulties have developed and organisations such as People First have sprung up and thrived.

Bringing notions of self-advocacy and informed individual choice into the initial assessment process for learners with learning difficulties is not always easy, particularly with learners who have little formal communication and difficulty in expressing concepts. It is also difficult for all adults who may not have experienced this style of adult education before. Gardner and Nudler (1997) establish three dimensions which must be satisfied if informed choices are to be made:

- if they are to make informed choices, people with learning difficulties need to have a range of concrete experiences in order to understand possible alternatives;

- they will need ongoing support in decision-making; and

- service providers will need to be able to suggest creative alternatives that satisfy the interests behind the choice.

There have been many publications written from a social services perspective on how to develop services based on individual peoples' aspirations (McIntosh, 1998; Wertheimer, 1996) and these refer to the role that education can play in helping people to find ways of fulfilling these aspirations. The Circles Network, a national voluntary organisation based around the key principles of inclusion and person-centred planning approaches, (**www.circlesnetwork.org.uk**) has developed ways of working with groups made up of family members and close friends of the person with a learning difficulty in order to discover more about their life-aims. Sutcliffe and Simons (1993) have looked at how education can support people in developing their self-advocacy skills. However, it is easy for staff to believe they are working from the perspective of what learners are saying they want while in fact not actually altering their traditional ways of working. This is particularly so when the learners are people with learning difficulties. As Simons (1998, p 267) says: if people are to be truly empowered through advocacy, service-providers need to change their attitudes so that they are 'working with people rather than doing things for them'.

One recent publication which looks specifically at how learner views and aspirations can form the focus for the learning programme, even with those young people and adults with the most profound learning difficulties, is *Enhancing Quality of Life: Facilitating Transitions for People with Profound and Complex Learning Difficulties* (Byers *et al.*, 2002). This pack was produced as the result of a three-year action research project with four sites – a further education college, a specialist college, an adult and community centre and a voluntary organisation. It contains a staff development pack, a literature review, guidance notes for policy makers and managers, a video and also a Quality of Life Audit (from Byers *et al.*, 2002). The last item provides a set of indicators grouped into five domains (Respect, Choices, Change, Feelings and Relationships) and gives service providers a framework against which they can evaluate, in relation to these domains, the quality of services they are providing for people with profound and complex learning difficulties.

Hopes, needs and aspirations

- All but four of the respondents to our questionnaire stated that learners had opportunities to state their needs and aspirations. Two questions were asked about systems of recording learning objectives, of which one directly asked respondents if they created Individual Learning Plans for learners with learning difficulties. Three providers – a sixth form college, a voluntary sector provider and a further education college – did not respond to this question; one further education college reported that ILPs were being developed; the remainder all said 'Yes'. However, three of the LEAs qualified their affirmation, two referring to them as 'records of work' and the other indicating some lack of confidence in the terminology:

  Yes (called record of work) (LEA)

  Yes; however we call them 'records of work'. This is deliberate. For me it is important that they are for learners and not bureaucratic purposes!!' (LEA)

  Yes, but I am not sure that our system records are what a large college would class as an ILP. We only offer part time adult education classes, put together to form a fairly cohesive plan. (LEA)

  The other question about learners recording needs and aspirations, asked respondents to describe how this was done. Here we discover that even more variations in terminology and alternative forms of learners' plans crop up, from 'Action Plans' to 'Records of Work' (see

Table 2. Variant terminology for, and alternative forms of, learners' plans

	Further education	LEA	Sixth form college	Specialist college	Voluntary sector	Work-based learning	WEA	Totals
Action Plans	2		3		2	1		8
Essential Skills Programme	1							1
Individual Learning Plans	32	4	7		1	1		45
Interview	2							2
Learning Agreement		1						1
Learning Goal Form	2						1	3
Learning Profile		1						1
No opportunity to meet individual needs					1			1
No recording system specified	6	2	1	1				10
None recorded			2					2
Person-Centred Plans	3		1		1			5
Personal Files	2							2
Progress File	1		1					2
Record of Work		2						2
Skill Plan	1							1
	52	10	15	1	5	2	1	86

Table 2), even from those respondents who said that they kept Individual Learning Plans. This may indicate that there is still a lot of confusion about what an individual learning plan is and how it should be kept, or that providers have retained or developed their own methods and models of recording learner information.

● We asked for some description of the types of Individual Learning Plan materials in use.

Interestingly, while many responded to say that they used in-house paper-based ILPs, others gave some clear insight into alternative approaches to identifying and assessing learners learning needs.

Prominent were those that used picture-based methods (photographs and symbols and widget technologies) and multi-media to facilitate learner choice.

specialised software, widget (rebus symbols) change picture bank (FE)

Two of the further education providers were experimenting with plans that could be accessed centrally on the computer from any classroom to enable them to be immediate and assessable.

One LEA used a combination of approaches:

Pictorial/photographic material. Offer taster sessions for learners to try something new. Trying out new systems using photographic labels for pre-literate learners. (LEA)

Simple texts, pictures, we are currently experimenting with several different formats. (Voluntary sector)

Specially designed coloured sheets with a spidergram (with the) student at (the) centre. (Sixth form college)

and the further education college where assessment was based on Person-centred Planning:

this still needs developing, but together with social services we are presently using our own designed PCP... (FE)

- We asked the respondents what types of learning outcomes they were monitoring and recording:

Table 3 captures all the learning monitored and recorded by the learning-providers who responded to our questionnaire.

However, many respondents both to our questionnaires and face-to-face encounters expressed concern about how to make these observations meaningful both to the learner and the learning-provider. Many commented that whilst self-esteem and self-confidence were recognised by teaching and support staff, they found it difficult to record progress or otherwise in a standardised way.

Table 3. Learning progress recognised by providers

	Sixth form colleges	Further education colleges	LEA	LEA/Work-based learning-provider	Specialist college	Voluntary organisation
Anger control		15				
Assertiveness		1				
Attendance/ Time keeping	1	7				1
Behaviour	1	11				
Citizenship	1	2				
Communication	1	8	3		1	1
Confidence	3	10	5			3
Empowerment			1			
Following instructions	1	1		1		
Independence/ travel	2	6	3		1	
Literacy/ numeracy	3	8	2			
Motivation		1	2			
Motor skills			1			
Participation/ commitment	1	3		1	1	
Personal development		3	2			
Presentation	1					
Safe working			1			
Self-esteem	1	4	1			1
Skills		8	1			
Social skills/group	3	30	2	1	1	2
Subject knowledge		4	1			
Trying	1					
Vocalisation/ gestures		2				
Vocational	1	5				
None	4	1	1	1		

Person-centred planning

When looking at ways in which listening to people with learning difficulties forms the basis for initial assessment and devising individualised programmes it is essential to examine *Valuing People: a new strategy for learning disability in the 21st Century* (DoH, 2000). Valuing People describes an initial assessment process which has as its basis the importance of listening to people with learning difficulties. This information is then used to support people in drawing up their own 'person-centred' plans.

'Towards Person-centred Approaches' (part of the *Valuing People* pack) contains an excellent review of resources, both publications and videos, which explain the concept and practice of person-centred planning. This work builds on a wealth of texts created by those working in social care on how to make action plans with people with learning difficulties. The central principle and value of person-centred planning is that it is the individual who is the focus of the plan. Individual learners, along with (where relevant) those people who care for them directly or indirectly and their close family or friends take a lead in deciding what is important for that individual. Important aims may be long-term or short-term. The aim of the person-centred plan is to find ways and means of meeting those goals, as opposed to the individual fitting in with an existing service or provision. Person-centred planning works from a value base that shifts the power of professionals and carers from that of power over the person to power alongside them. It encourages two questions to be addressed to the individual: 'who are you and who are we in your life?' and 'what can we do together to achieve a better life for you now and in the future?' (Sanderson, 2000). Not only does this give clear messages for partnership approaches to working, but also offers avenues of opportunity for teachers and learning-providers to identify learning needs and aspirations. Whilst advice might be sought from a range of professionals, their opinions may not necessarily be adopted. In other words planning may be outside 'the box' of what is provided, and what is available.

Black (2000) notes that following a person-centred approach requires service providers to take on the values of 'inclusion', to be creative and acknowledge risk.

> *We have found that person-centred planning works, because it is rooted in the values of inclusion, will always require participants to work outside of service-land and in the real world. This means that providers must think really carefully about keeping people safe whilst enabling the risk taking which is a part of all our lives* (Black, 2000, 8: 8).

Valuing People (DoH 2000) has much relevance to staff supporting learners with learning difficulties and have to devise a person-centred curriculum. However, people working in educational settings often do not make use of it. Education practitioners are often unaware of the wealth of guidance material available on person-centred planning, and there is often little opportunity for them to work with other agencies to look at how an educational programme can relate to an individual's overall plan.

Person-centred planning – survey findings

Fifty-four respondents said that they were not involved in person-centred planning; six of these stated that they had not heard of it. Twenty-seven respondents stated that they were involved to some extent in person-centred panning processes, and a further four were waiting for training. It is possible that the number who do not know what it is could be even higher, as a number of the responses indicated that 'person-centred planning' was interpreted as learner-centred planning:

> *yes, if you mean ILP'S* (FE)

or

> *'I don't know what you mean. If you mean individually tailored programmes of support, then we have done this for the last 13 years'* (LEA)

or

> *'unsure as to the current definition of person-centred planning'* (FE)

One of the further education colleges appeared to receive instructions only in relation to personal care:

> '(p.c.p.) *only for learners with more complex personal care or medical needs* (college's involvement in p.c.p.) *only in carrying out personal care/ medical procedures…'* (FE).

From those few providers who made a remark about person-centred planning, it was clear that it was not well understood and that it was only partially implemented. There were also two areas of discontent about person-centred plans. One was lack of time to be involved in what was viewed as a time-consuming activity. The other was a perceived lack of information from social services departments.

Table 4. Providers' involvement in person-centred planning

Provider type	No response	Involved in person-centred planning	Aware of person-centred planning and awaiting training in	Not involved	Not heard of person-centred planning	Totals
LEA		2	1	6	1	10
LEA/work-based learning				3		3
Sixth form colleges	1	2		10	1	14
Voluntary organisations		2		3	3	8
Further Education College		21	3	25	1	50
Specialist College	1					1
WEA				1		1
Totals	**2**	**27**	**4**	**48**	**6**	**87**

Working with others

The sections above show how important it is for education staff to work with others if they are to fully explore individual aspirations. This is even more important for those working with people with learning difficulties. Learners with learning difficulties are more likely to be receiving support from a variety of agencies, hence initial assessment needs to be informed by close collaboration between different agencies. However, structural difficulties often mean that this does not occur (Byers *et al.*, 2002). Literature on collaborative working (Lacey and Lomas, 1993; Lacey, 2001) shows both the difficulties faced when services try to collaborate and also some strategies for overcoming these blocks. McIntosh and Whittaker (2000) in their study of people with complex learning difficulties, emphasise how collaborative approaches between agencies are essential, particularly when working with those who have more complex needs.

The texts cited above list some of the blocks that thwart close collaboration between agencies. These include:

● a lack of understanding of what the other agency does and how it works;

- a lack of time and training for staff to carry out essential collaborative work;

- concerns over who should fund what – exacerbated when resources are short; and

- questions of ownership, with each agency feeling they should be taking the lead.

Staff can also find that concern over confidentiality prevents agencies from sharing important information. Of course it is essential that learners should give expressed consent to staff sharing information. However, both Lacey (2001) and the writers of Enhancing Quality of Life (Byers *et al.*, 2002) reveal that sometimes the issue of confidentiality can be used as an excuse for lack of collaboration rather than being a real block.

Involving others – survey findings

In our questionnaire we asked if Individual Learning Plans (ILPs) were shared with other agencies, carers or friends. Five providers did not respond to this. Twenty-three respondents said no, seven explained this further by citing (as mentioned above) data-protection issues and confidentiality:

No, (the) material remains confidential – only with consent of the learner in reviews etc. (FE)

No this is personal and confidential (FE)

One respondent interestingly suggested that the purpose of the ILP was primarily for inspection purposes:

No, Learning Plan has to be available to satisfy OFSTED etc. Not usually shown to any one else other than lecturer or tutors (Sixth form colleges)

The remainder answered 'Yes' and stated who they shared this with. Most respondents added that permission was sought from the learner first. They were shared with:

- parents and guardians;
- day centres and social services; and
- Connexions and employment advisers.

If teaching staff are to respond fully to the individual aspirations of people with learning difficulties they will need to work far more closely with other agencies. Managers will need to recognise and allocate the time needed to do this. Learning-providers will need to be clear about what their role can be in supporting the fulfilment of individual, person-centred plans. This is particularly true in the light of *Valuing People*'s expressed aim to 'modernise day services', by which they often mean the closing of traditional day centres and the inclusion of people within the community. Important as this aim is, it has left some educational providers concerned that, in the absence of traditional provision, they will 'become the new day centre'. Such an outcome would certainly not be in the best interests of people with learning difficulties, and an appropriate response requires close liaison between education and other providers in order to be clear exactly how education providers can best fit into this new situation. As well as working closely with other agencies it is likely that education providers will also need to be far more flexible in their ways of working and accept that their usual model of a fixed-time, standard learning programme may not necessarily be the most effective way of responding to individual aims (NIACE, *Two Briefing Papers on Valuing People*, 2001).

The *QCA/DfEE Guidance* (QCA, 2002) gives examples of how information can be shared in order to explore more fully what learners really want. With young adults there is a structure for carrying this out in the form of the Transition Plan which has to be produced for young people, together with a statement of educational need. It is the statutory duty of the Connexions Service to produce a written assessment of need for learners with a statement of educational need as they leave school (Learning and Skills Act 2000, Section 140). However, with adult learners the structures for collaboration are less clear and more ad hoc. Working with others does not just include working with statutory agencies but also the possibility of working with learners' friends and family. The Circle of Friends methodology (**www.circlesnetwork.org.uk**) has developed ways of creating such circles of support while putting the person with a learning difficulty firmly at the centre of the process.

Working with others – survey findings

- In our questionnaire we asked respondents how they planned and assessed learning with other agencies and organisations. A majority of the respondents cited their contact with other agencies as being at times of transition, most commonly from school. The agency most often reported as working with learning-providers was Connexions (seventeen responders). The respondents referred to a wide range of agencies or places that they liaised with including day centres (eight responses), nurses and social workers (fourteen responses), employers in connection with work-based learning programmes (three responses) and specialist services such as speech therapy, psychology and support charities (seven responses). Two responders reported that they did not work with others. One of the further education colleges felt that they did 'not (work) very well' with others.

- Respondents also told us about the extent to which families were involved in reporting and sharing change and progression; this is reported in section 4.

(3) Learning objectives

The third stage of the RARPA process is concerned with Identification of learning objectives which meet the stated outcomes of the programme of learning, the learner group and the individual learner.

Much of the literature cited earlier examines ways in which initial identification of an individual's aspirations can then be broken down into specific, tangible objectives.

Course development – survey findings

- Our questionnaire asked how learners' hopes and aspirations were incorporated into learning programmes. A range of approaches was reported. Generally, most providers indicated that they set a range of short-term and long-term goals for their learners and shared these with tutors and support workers.

   They are completed with the learner and based on initial assessment. They are then used to inform the learning programme by a series of targets which are reviewed mid-term and at the end of the learning programme. (Work-based learning)

- Otherwise, responses were divided into those which, like the example above, set goals and targets for learners to meet, and those where the courses were individually tailored to meet need:

   For example, if a student indicates that they would like to be an independent traveller – we work towards this goal and incorporate travel skills into many curriculum areas. If, however, a student indicates that he wants to be a policeman we would address this in tutorial – as part of a wider discussion about post-college placements. Hopes and aspirations of a personal nature, e.g. getting married, are discussed in tutorial. (FE)

and introducing specific schemes of work like the ASDAN (**www.asdan.co.uk**) and Essential Skills Award (Mencap, 2001).

By introducing ASDAN modules to closely match their aspirations, e.g. to live independently – cookery, everyday living skills and setting small achievable goals to work towards aspiration. (FE)

Action plan based on these followed by subject tutor who set SMART targets, using Essential Skills Awards (MENCAP). (FE)

- Most of the responders referred to the necessity of making resources (extra support, materials and equipment) flexible and mobile. Ensuring through their proper use that courses met learners' needs.

Two responders suggested that the learners had to choose the right course to meet their individual needs, rather than the education providers setting one to meet the individual needs of the learners.

Core programme offered is very specific, centred around supported work experience and vocational preparation. We ensure learners have made an informed choice to enter it by having a 6-week mutual trial period at start. (Voluntary Sector)

QCA Guidance (2002) and *Enhancing Quality of Life* (Byers *et al.*, 2002) look specifically at how aspirations can be translated into particular educational goals. The QCA Guidance, in its excellent case studies, gives clear examples of positive ways in which this can occur with a range of learners with learning difficulties studying on very varied programmes. For example: a student's stated aspiration is to set up a youth club and organise leisure activities for other people. He would also like a job. In the example, staff look with him at the skills he would need to begin to meet these, which include using a headswitch to increase his communication and hence his autonomy, developing his ability to work within a group and taking a greater part in planning his own learning. They then find ways to meet these objectives within his learning context. This includes both simulations and role-play and also real life experiences such as showing visitors around the college, running a 'tuck shop' with other learners and becoming a representative on the Students Union. (*QCA Guidance*, 2002, case study).

However, it is clear that this is an area which still requires considerable development. Teachers working with adults with learning difficulties may discuss initial aspirations but then not collaborate closely enough with the learner in setting up ways to work towards these goals in an educational context. This can leave learners unclear as to how the tasks staff ask them to do in class really further their aims. A recent LSDA publication, *Count me in FE* (Anderson, 2003) gives the results of a number of interviews with college students with learning difficulties and shows how many of those on discrete learning programmes 'were not clear about how their programmes met their learning goals and how these linked to their aspirations' (p 36). Assessment with adults with learning difficulties needs to be seen as an ongoing process. Too often teachers may work closely with learners in eliciting their overall aspirations but then devise their own objectives as to how those aspirations might best be responded to in a teaching situation. Hence, what starts off as an interactive and constructive approach reverts to a behaviourist method of teaching.

The Tomlinson Report (FEFC, 1996) shows clearly that *what* is taught cannot be separated from *how* it is taught and how learners learn, and that focus on learning content must be paralleled by a focus on learning styles and preferences. Babbage, Byers and Redding (1999) emphasise the importance of continually involving learners with learning difficulties in assessing how they learn best; they have produced useful Learning Profile Sheets in which learners and staff can work together to identify areas in which learners feel at ease and areas in which they experience frustration and stress. Lawson (1992, 1998) has also looked at how staff can use the tutorial process and self-recording sheets to encourage adults with learning difficulties to become more aware of their strengths as learners and understand the particular contexts in which they learn best.

Learning styles – survey findings

- Our questionnaire asked how learning-providers identified the learning styles of adults with learning difficulties.

  Four providers did not respond and three stated that they were experiencing various degrees of difficulty:

  This is not done formally at present. Tutors recognise that different learning styles exist, and use many different ways to approach learning with a group, e.g. visual, audio, creative, practical. Over a period of time with a group the tutor will be able to identify how individuals best learn and respond. (Work-based learning)

  Initially tried this by asking them to tick boxes (with visual prompts) didn't work. Don't anymore (LEA)

  Not very well! Software available in all centres but rarely used (LEA)

- Generally, learning style questionnaires and classroom-based observation were the most usual methods of assessing learning styles. Three providers presented the learners with a variety of different teaching approaches or projects and observed which method they responded to well:

By offering a range of opportunities for the learner to work on different projects and resolving which style(s) appear to be the most useful (Work-based learning)

Through experimentation, observation and discussion. Often people are not aware of having a preferred learning style when they begin a course with us, having always been unsuccessful. (Voluntary sector)

Observation, level of engagement, willingness to participate in activities. (FE)

Table 5. The range of methods used to identify learning styles. Many respondents indicated several methods

	Question-naires	Observation	Practical in classroom	Interview	Taster programme
FE college	22	17		9	3
LEA	4	4	1		
Sixth form colleges	9	4		1	
Specialist college				1	1
Voluntary Organisation	1	2	1		
Work-based learning			1		

4 Formative assessment

The fourth RARPA stage concerns formative assessment, where the evidence gained by assessment is 'actually used to adapt teaching to meet students' needs' (Black and Wiliam, 1998).

Recently there has been considerable focus on standardised tests and summative assessment, which tries to discover what a particular learner knows. A strict adherence to this approach denies the importance of formative assessment, in which the evidence discovered by assessment is used to make changes to the learning situation. Several studies have shown how improved formative assessment has a quantifiable positive effect on raising standards (Black and Wiliam, 1998). Vorhaus (2000) shows how formative assessment, with its 'future-regarding perspective' is particularly appropriate for adult learners as opposed to summative assessment 'which takes the form of a global retrospective judgement'. Particularly important for this review, Black and Wiliam note that many studies (e.g. Fuchs *et al.*, 1997) have shown that 'improved formative assessment helps low achievers more than other students and so reduces the range of achievement while raising achievement overall'.

Effective formative assessment allows learners the space to talk about their learning and express their own learning goals. It requires staff to spend more time listening and observing. It also requires 'divergent assessment' which emphasises what the learner knows, can do and can understand rather than 'convergent assessment' which relies on closed questioning and tasks (Torrance and Pryor, 2001).

Such approaches reflect a constructionist rather than a behaviourist approach to assessment and are particularly appropriate for learners with a learning difficulty. However, as Ecclestone (2002) points out, staff in post-school education do not always 'appreciate the need to understand theories about assessment and then relate them to changes in practice', and if this is the case 'formative assessment is little more than continuous summative assessment.

Recording – survey findings

- Respondents recorded progress on Individual Learning Plans or the equivalent. Three of the respondents specifically referred to portfolios and photographic recording of progress:

Photographs. Individual learners own work – portfolios. Learner self-evaluation. Evaluation forms tailored to each course and characteristics of each learner groups. (LEA)

Portfolios, tracking records, reports from tutors, weekly records, LSA records. (FE)

- Individual responses referred to how often the ILPs were reviewed. From daily (specialist college) to weekly, more commonly monthly (thirty respondents) and termly. Some of the learning-providers reported mixed methods for recording and monitoring learner progress:

The tutor, in negotiation with the learner, sets targets to be achieved within a certain period of time. A record of what the student does during each session is noted in the student work record (aims, methods and resources, learning outcomes, and follow up) which is an intrinsic part of the ILP. Progress is then monitored through continuous assessment and when the learner achieves his/her target, a record of this is made in the ILP. Once a term, the learner has a learning review meeting with the tutor to discuss progress. (FE)

By means of assessments linked to individual learning plans; self-assessment exercises; revision exercises; regular updates on learner's progress through milestones in the pre-entry curriculum; half-termly review and renegotiation of the individual learning plans. Termly progress review/interview bringing together all learning programmes.' (LEA)

In most groups, where learning is in 'small steps', individual targets/student progress towards these are recorded on lesson plans. Targets are reviewed by course teams at least termly and in some cases more frequently, as a result of which individual targets are re-set. Course teams meet frequently and there is much informal discussion. (FE)

One of the sixth form colleges reported that they were more likely to record academic progress only and no other outcomes:

Tutors record progress but are more likely to record progress in terms of progress towards academic or skills targets not softer targets e.g. confidence or self-esteem. (Sixth form college)

Involving families – survey findings

- We asked in our questionnaire how families and friends might be involved in reporting change to the learning-providers in order to provide formative evidence.

Three said that they don't generally ask for information because of data-protection issues:

They don't! Our contract is with the learner and we comply with Data Protection principles. We have participated in and contributed to total care plans but only with the learner's permission. (LEA)

The ways in which parents, carers and friends could communicate with providers varied. Two providers were pro-active and regularly contacted parents and carers to check progress. Fourteen providers expected parents/friends and carers to contact them. Five providers referred to two-way communication through the use of diaries or communication books. Two respondents reported that parents and carers are invited to social service reviews, twenty invited them to college reviews.

At present this is an area that is underdeveloped, although carers are encouraged to feedback improvement. (LEA)

We have no formal way for family/friends to report change. Depending on the nature of the change, the families or friends of the learner get in touch directly with us or contact the Department for Learning Support (Disabilities) if that is more appropriate. The information is then passed onto us on a 'need to know' basis. (FE)

Regular parents' evenings, letters to home advising of the progress of students and upcoming events. Parents/carers are actively encouraged to keep close contact with the personal tutor. (FE)

Currently not involved unless they take initiative. Families and friends are not overly encouraged or discouraged to become involved' (Sixth form college)

5 Recognising progress and achievement

The final part of the RARPA five-stage process is the end of programme assessments and review of overall progress and achievement. The guidance from the LSC (2003) based on ALI guidance, suggests that evidence of progress and achievement is captured in a wide range of formats: 'learners' files, journals, diaries, portfolios, artwork; videos, audiotapes, performances, exhibitions and displays; individual or group learner testimony; artefacts, photographs and other forms of evidence.'

Nashashibi (2002b, p 5) states that:

> *Achievement in learning means increased skill, knowledge and understanding. It is many faceted. The richness of a successful learning experience and the gains to individuals and groups cannot all be defined. We recognise the impact in use and enjoyment. While a sense of achievement, and the potential to do more, comes with successful learning, learners sometimes undervalue their achievements and do not gain the confidence they need to move on. Assessment is a means of analysing learning, enabling learners to see their progress, gain confidence and build on it – to recognise it more fully.*

So it is successful learning that we are hoping to recognise, both for the learning-providers' sake as well as the learners'. Without it, it is impossible to understand how to improve provision and recognise good practice, and, as Nashashibi suggests, it is difficult for the learner to progress.

Cautionary notes, however, have been sounded about how achievements are reported to learners. Rather than encourage more learning activity, positive reinforcement can (in children) have a detrimental effect, leading to task-avoidance or caution for fear of failure (Ames 1984; Dwerk 1989). Weiner (1984) goes on to suggest that learners can hold themselves entirely responsible for their own success or failure. Failing to recognise that external factors such as the learning institution, learning objectives or teaching methodology may also be part of the overall success/failure equation, could, affect their self-esteem or confidence. Further to this, Weiner (1984) pointed out that learners may go on to believe either that they are successful or failures consistently in one event or domain (e.g. maths or written exams), or that their success or failure is applicable to everything that they do. It is clear, then, that practitioners working with learners at all levels need to be in tune with the learners' aspirations and learning styles in order to recognise their achievements effectively.

Recent literature often refers to the term 'distance travelled' as a way of identifying learner achievement. In order to recognise these 'distance travelled' achievements, robust approaches need to be in place to help the learner and the practitioner identify 'where they are now' at the beginning of a programme of learning so that they can identify where it is they have reached. This methodology should also be applied with caution, bearing in mind that learners achieve unexpected learning outcomes. An account of a supported learning project in Sheffield (Booth and Booth, 2003) demonstrates the importance of being aware of other learning gains. The project aimed to provide personal support and self-advocacy development to mothers with learning difficulties to support their parenting and their ability to meet the needs of their children. Many of the outcomes, including basic skills progress, were measured and accredited. The report writers, however, felt that the confidence gained by one mother with a 'long personal history of passivity and acquiescence' to make a complaint to her dentist '…might signify the greater achievement'.

Recognising achievement – survey findings

Achievements were recognised in a number of ways by our questionnaire respondents:

- Certificates

  If students progress and are enjoying their learning experience we produce a college certificate which states on reverse the achievement of the student. (FE)

- Reports

- Taking records of work home

- Verbal reports

- Displays of files and photographs

- Open Days and Award Evenings

  Award evenings, shows, student reps. (FE)

  Learners receive recognition at Graduation from the course and in their final progress report. (FE)

- Performances

  There is plenty of room for display of artefacts and artwork of all types in the college, and performance spaces for suitable events. (LEA)

- Presentations

  Celebration of success in class by making presentations of work. For instance, inviting guests to lunch in a cookery class, organising displays of art and craft work, giving a drama performance, a group making a presentation of a project. Lots of photos and displays. (LEA)

and many who showed through their responses multiple approaches:

Achievements are recognised and celebrated in the group or one-to-one. Effort can be recognised and recorded in the form of in-house certificates an presentation ceremonies. Recognition of achievement is marked by review of personal targets and new target-setting. (Sixth form college)

Barriers and opportunities for good practice – survey findings

In order to enable opportunities for good practice in recognizing progress and achievement in non-accredited learning to flourish it is essential that barriers and opportunities are recognised.

Finally, we asked the respondents to our questionnaire what they perceived to be the barriers, benefits and opportunities are for recognising and recording non-accredited achievements of learners with learning difficulties. Fourteen respondents did not respond to this question, and eight said there were no barriers.

The barriers identified were:

Funding

Some providers believed that it was difficult to obtain funding for non-accredited provision, others believed that the problem lay with the LSC having poor knowledge about recording achievement.

Lack of integrated presentation evenings now that the college has merged (now under review from SMT, after concerns were expressed). Lack of understanding of issues by LSC and greater flexibility and acceptance of value added to be recognised. (FE)

None in own organisation, but it is felt that LSC is moving towards accreditation and away from ' other provision (FE)

Time

Many providers (16) felt that there was no extra time available to record and monitor non-accredited progress and achievement.

Nearly all classes staffed by p/t tutors whose contracts stipulate student contact time only. Union agreement that p/t staff should not assume other duties. (FE)

The time involved in doing this in a meaningful way. Making such recording accessible to the students themselves. (LEA)

Shortage of tutor time. We always try to give learners feedback on and praise for their achievements, but we don't always record this. (Voluntary sector)

Time – the learners are on site for such a small amount of time (two and five hours) it is not practical to expect tutors to record soft skill achievements consistently. (FE)

One of the respondents felt that more administrative support would help.

Process

Here we have identified internal management processes, some of the providers felt that the management recording processes were not friendly to non-accredited learning outcomes:

The college system for recording achievement is inflexible. (FE)

and processes for tutors to recognise and record achievement. Some expressed concern about how they could 'quantify' achievement, since they believed that this was expected of them:

Methods which are recognised or that can be measured as they are soft outcomes – (this is not just an organisational barrier). Data systems that are used to capture achievement. (FE)

Staff knowledge and attitudes

Twelve respondents recorded their concerns that staff lacked knowledge about non-accredited processes:

Difficulties of detailed initial assessment, e.g. on learning styles/basic skills etc – this is time-consuming and unmanageable within our staffing levels and the p/t nature of our provision and staff. Staff training in recording achievement still on-going, with patchy results. (LEA)

Perception that such achievements will not attract funding (or appear in league tables). (Sixth form colleges)

including management knowledge:

Ensuring MIS/exams understand that we work in small steps and any achievement can be recognised and recorded. Not just full qualifications. (FE)

and coupled with this that some staff attitudes towards change was poor:

Outside the discrete programme. I would say it is staff's attitude – more by ignorance I think: also the attitude that 'this is the way I have always done things!'.(FE)

Benefits and opportunities – survey findings

Respondents identified opportunities arising from recognising non-accredited learning.

Learner centred

Twenty-five of the comments reflected that participating in non-accredited learning has improved the provision and quality of learner-centred work. This includes using local resources more effectively. Also that small-step learning was increasingly recognised. From this, many indicated that curriculum planning was improved and that learners were made better learning offers.

Offering appropriate provision. Establishing a long-term goal. Listening and responding to the learners needs. Establishing appropriate support. Identifying progression opportunities. Developing provision in accordance with student need. (LEA)

They learn what they need to learn. Lecturers encouraged to teach the student not just the subject. (FE)

We need to do this if we are to be inclusive in our approach. We see the person as an 'individual' – too often our learners are seen as 'groups'. We need to know 'the needs' to be able to put in effective support. (LEA)

Staff involvement

Ten of the respondents referred to the quality of staff, including interest and flexibility of individuals as being key to the development of recognising non-accredited learning and to its maintenance.

Management

Three of the respondents felt that the management staff of their provision were supportive and helped enable these programmes to develop.

None in own organisation, but it is felt that LSC is moving towards accreditation and away from 'other provision'. (FE)

Staffing – time resource to attend reviews etc. Staff absence/changes have delayed developments. Disproportionate number of part-time agency staff meaning training, awareness raising difficult. (FE)

Funding from LSC. Currently claiming as Basic Skills (1.4) but have constant battle to justify that pre-entry work is basic skills. (FE)

Empowerment and involvement

Respondents wrote about how they believed that learners had a stronger sense of ownership of their learning by identifying their hopes and aspirations.

Learners 'own' their learning programme, it ensures progression and helps individuals reach targets. (Work-based learning)

Learners have ownership of their own learning. They can learn at their own pace. A more imaginative and flexible framework of learning is established. (FE)

It is important to treat each student as an individual and to ensure that the learning programme is devised to meet their individual learning needs. Learning support must be put in place in order to ensure that each student is given the opportunity to optimise their potential. For many students this process of identifying individual aspirations and learning needs will be the first time that they have been treated as adults and really listened to. This is sure to impact on their feeling of self-worth and result in a positive attitude towards their education. They are learning for themselves, not because someone has told them they need to do it. (FE)

Relevance and meaningfulness

Some of the responses indicated that learner-centred approaches had led to an improved relationship between the learner and the curriculum:

'There is a better approach to the delivery of programmes because there is more chance that the programme is relevant to the individual.' (Work-based learning)

Promoting confidence and enjoyment

Many of the respondents felt that identifying aspirations and seeing them incorporated into the learning programmes led to a positive outcome of increased confidence itself.

Progression and retention

A key benefit identified by nine of the respondents was that they felt that learners were able to progress more sensibly as a result of identifying hopes and aspirations:

This allows us to look at transitional planning and to adapt our provision. (FE)

and that retention rates were improved because learners were experiencing more rewarding learning experiences:

To ensure students are on the appropriate course at the appropriate level; to keep them focussed, committed and working towards their personal goals. (FE)

As with all our courses it will help to ensure that the course content is relevant and appropriate. Learners will be more likely to complete the course and to progress onto others. Contributes a positive and valuing experience to learners. (LEA)

Conclusion

One of the very positive discoveries in this piece of work was the enthusiasm with which providers responded to the questionnaire. Eighty-seven people completed the questionnaires. Many individuals rang in to say they hoped they could still respond even though the deadline had passed because they realised how important this approach was. It is clear that many providers are strongly committed to finding appropriate and innovative ways of devising curricula based on the individual aspirations and needs of learners with learning difficulties and finding appropriate ways of recording their progress and achievement. However, it is still apparent that much of this work is piecemeal and does not adhere to an overall institutional and sector response. Respondents spoke of the difficulty, even within a single organisation, of ensuring that their approach was shared by all staff, and of the particular difficulties of getting consistency when they made use of a large number of part-time tutors.

It was also clear that many of those who responded found it hard to fit their approach into management systems of recording progress, which they did not always find 'friendly to non-accredited learning'. There appears to be a persistent belief held by certain managers that this kind of approach to learning will not attract funding and a pressure to fit learners with learning difficulties into an outcome-related curriculum of basic skills teaching. These perceptions can easily lead onto a 'checklist' mentality whereby rigid, teacher-led outcomes can take the place of learning which is genuinely student-led and based on learner aspirations.

There is also a further issue in that the value given to external accreditation and more tangible outcomes can then become expressed in learners' own stated aims. In the section on E2E above (p 17) we saw how learners themselves often wanted official accreditation even when this was not necessarily the best way of fulfilling their own aspirations. Similarly, some learners with learning difficulties will state their desire 'to learn reading and writing' because of its perceived status, whereas a focus on other wider skills might lead more appropriately to fulfilment of their overall aim. This tension reflects the need for far more status to be given to areas of learning which are not formally accredited.

In terms of the literature search it was interesting to see how much innovative work in the area of devising individual plans for people with learning difficulties has taken place outside the educational sector. However, questionnaire results showed that many respondents were either unaware of this or did not have a real understanding of the concept of person-centred planning. Our study led to the firm conclusion that there needs to be far more opportunity for sharing between different agencies and a greater understanding of how post-school education fits into new developments, as articulated in Valuing People.

The literature search also revealed the lack of a fully worked-out theoretical underpinning for post-school work with learners with learning difficulties. Extremely important and valuable guidance documents have been produced for the post-school sector. However, the major theoretical developments dealing with assessment of learners with learning difficulties has occurred in the school, rather than the post-school, sector. It appears that two conclusions need to be drawn from this. The first is that post-school education for learners with learning difficulties does have a lot to learn from this school-based work. Too often there can be an approach which dismisses any school-based theories as irrelevant to post-school learning. The second is that of course there are differences in adult learning. There needs to be more understanding of the ways in which adults with learning difficulties learn, so that a theoretical framework can be developed to underpin practical developments in post-school work with learners with learning difficulties.

References

Acts of Parliament:

Disability Discrimination Act 1995, London: HMSO

Learning and Skills Act 2000, London, The Stationery Office.

Special Educational Needs and Disability Act 2001, London, The Stationery Office.

Ames, C. (1984). 'Comparative, co-operative and individualistic goal structures: a motivational analysis', in Ames, R. and Ames C., *Research on Motivation in Education*, Orlando, Academic Press.

Anderson, V., Faraday, S., Prowse, S., Richards, G. and Swindells, D. (2003). *Count me in FE*, London, LSDA.

Association of Colleges (2002). *Rights of Access – A Toolkit to Help Colleges Meet or Exceed the Requirements of DDA Part 4*, London, AoC.

Babbage, R., Byers, R., Redding, H. (1999). *Approaches to Teaching and Learning: Including Pupils with Learning Difficulties*, London, David Fulton Publishers.

Basic Skills Agency (2001). *Pre Entry Curriculum Framework for Literacy and Numeracy*, London, Basic Skills Agency Publications.

Baxter, L. (2001). *The Adult Community College Colchester: Measuring Achievement of Non-accredited Learning (A case study of the Adult and Community Learning Quality Support Programme)*, London, LSDA/NIACE, **www.qualityacl.org.uk**

Black, P. (2000). *Why aren't Person-centred Approaches and Planning Happening for as Many People as Well as We Would Like?* Joseph Rowntree Foundation Bulletins, York, Joseph Rowntree Foundation.

Black, P. and Wiliam, D. (1998). *Inside the Black Box: Raising Standards Through Classroom Assessment*, **www.pdkintl.org/kappan/kbla9810.htm**

Booth, T. and Booth, W. (2003). *Self-advocacy and Supported Learning for Mothers with Learning Difficulties* (Final project report for DfEE's Adult and Community Learning Fund), Sheffield, Supported Parenting and Sheffield Women's Cultural Club, **www.supported-parenting.com/projects/SLPpaper-final-copy.pdf**

Byers, R., Dee, L., Hayhoe, H. and Maudslay, L. (2002). *Enhancing Quality of Life: Facilitating Transitions for People with Profound and Complex Learning Difficulties*, London, SKILL.

Cline, T. (1992) (ed). *The Assessment of Special Educational Needs: International Perspectives*, London, Routledge.

Corbett, J. (1989). 'The Quality of Life in the "Independence" Curriculum', *Disability, Handicap and Society*, vol. 4, No. 2, pp 145–63.

Daniels, H. (1992). *Charting the Agenda: Educational Activity after Vygotsky*, London, Routledge.

Dee, L. (1999). 'Inclusive Learning. From Rhetoric to Reality', In Green, A. and Lucas, N. (eds) *FE and Lifelong Learning: Redesigning the Sector for the Twenty-first Century*, London: Bedford Way Papers, pp 139–60

Department for Education and Skills (2002a). *Guidance for LEAs and Adult Education Providers on Implementation of DDA Part 4*, London, DfES

Department for Education and Skills (2002b). *Adult Pre-entry Curriculum Framework for Literacy and Numeracy*, London, DfES

Department for Education and Skills (2003). *New Rights to Learn. A Tutor Guide to Teaching Adults after the Disability Discrimination Act Part 4*, London, NIACE.

Department of Health, (2000). *Valuing People: A New Strategy for Learning Disability in the 21st Century* (includes *Planning with People: Towards Person-centred Approaches*), London, DoH.

Dewson, S., Eccles, J., Tackey, N.D. and Jackson, A. (2000). *Measuring Soft Outcomes and Distance Travelled: A Review of Current Practice*, DfEE Research Report No. 219, London, DfES.

Disability Rights Commission (2002). *Code of Practice Post-16: Disability Discrimination Act 1995: Part 4.*

Dwerk, C. (1989). 'Motivation', in Lesgola, A. and Glaser, R., *Foundation for a Psychology of Education*, Hillsdale, Erlbaum.

Ecclestone, K. (2002). *Learning Autonomy in Post-16 Education: The Politics and Practice of Formative Assessment*, London, Routledge.

Frederickson, N. and Cline, T. (2003). *Special Educational Needs, Inclusion and Diversity: A Textbook*, Buckingham, Open University Press.

Fuchs, L.S., Fuchs, D., Karns, K., Hamlett, C.L., Katzaroff, M. and Dutka, S. (1997). 'Effects of task-focused goals in low-achieving students with and without learning disabilities', *American Educational Research Journal*, vol. 34, no. 3, pp513–43.

Further Education Funding Council (1996). *[The Tomlinson Report] Inclusive Learning: Report of the Learning Difficulties and/or Disabilities Committee*, London, HMSO.

Further Education Funding Council (1999). *National Awards for Students with Learning Difficulties*, London, HMSO

Gardner, J.F. and Nudler, S. (1997). 'Beyond compliance to responsiveness: accreditation reconsidered', in Schalock, R.L. (ed) *Quality of Life Volume 11: Application to Persons with Disabilities*, Washington DC: American Association on Mental Retardation.

Gickling, E.E. & Thompson, V.P. (1985). 'A personal view of curriculum-based assessments', *Exceptional Children*, vol. 52(3): 205–18.

Greenwood, M., Hayes, A., Turner, C. and Vorhaus, J. (2001). *Recognising and Validating Outcomes of Non-accredited Learning: A Practical Approach*, London, LSDA.

Grief S. and Windsor B. (2003). *Recognising and Validating Learning Outcomes and Achievements in Non-accredited Basic Skills and ESOL*, London, LSDA, **www.lsda.org.uk/files/lsda/currciulum/basicskills/1328.pdf**

James, M. (1998). *Using Assessment for School Improvement*, Oxford, Heinemann Educational Publishers.

Lacey, P. (2001). *Support Partnerships – Collaboration in Action*, London, David Fulton Publishers.

Lacey, P. and Lomas, J. (1993). *Supporting Services and the Curriculum – A Practical Guide to Collaboration*, London, David Fulton Publishers.

Lawson, H. (1992). *Practical Record Keeping for Special Schools: Resource Material for Staff Development*, London, David Fulton Publishers

Lawson, H. (1998). *Practical Record Keeping: Development and Resource Material for Staff Working with Pupils with Special Educational Needs* (second edition), London, David Fulton Publishers.

Learning and Skills Council (2002). *Framework for Entry to Employment Programmes*, London, LSC

Learning and Skills Council (2003). *LSC Position Paper on Recognising and Recording Progress and Achievement in Non-accredited Learning*, Coventry, LSC

Lunt, I (1992). 'The practice of assessment', in Daniels, H. (ed) *Charting the Agenda: Educational Activity after Vygotsky*, London, Routledge.

McIntosh, B. and Whittaker, A. (eds) (1998). *Days of Change: A Practical Guide to Developing Better Day Opportunities with People with Learning Difficulties*, London, Kings Fund.

McIntosh, B. and Whittaker, A. (eds) (2000). *Unlocking the Future – Developing New Lifestyles with People who have Complex Disabilities*, Kings Fund, London.

Mencap (2001). *The Essential Skills Award*, London, Mencap National College.

Nashashibi, P. (2002). *Learning in Progress; Recognising Achievement in Adult Learning*, London, LSDA.

NIACE (2001). *Valuing People: A New Strategy for Learning Disability for the 21st Century – A briefing paper for staff working in adult and further education, and Valuing People: Briefing paper for Learning Disability Partnership Boards*, Leicester, NIACE, **www.niace.org.uk**

Ouvry, C. and Saunders, S. (2001). 'Pupils with profound and multiple learning difficulties', in B. Carpenter, R. Ashdown and K. Boviar (eds) *Enabling Access: Effective Teaching and Learning for Pupils with Learning Difficulties* (second edition), London, David Fulton Publishers.

Qualifications and Curriculum Authority Guidance (2002): *Designing a Learner-centred Curriculum for 16–24 year olds with Learning Difficulties*, **www.qca.org.uk**

Qualifications and Curriculum Authority/Department for Education and Employment (2001). *Planning, Teaching and Assessing the Curriculum for Pupils with Learning Difficulties: General Guidelines*, London, QCA.

Sanderson, H. (2000). *Person-centred Planning: Key Features and Approaches*, Joseph Rowntree Foundation Bulletin, York, Joseph Rowntree Foundation.

Simons, K. (1998). 'What really matters? – helping people with learning difficulties to shape services', in Ward, L. (ed) *Innovations in Advocacy and Empowerment for People with Intellectual Disabilities*, Chorley, Lancs., Lisieux Hall.

Skill (2003). *Aasha: Working with Young People with a Learning Difficulty from a South Asian Background*, London, SKILL.

Sutcliffe, J. and Jacobsen, Y (1998). *All Things Being Equal? A Practical Guide to Widening Participation for Adults with Learning Difficulties in Continuing Education*, Leicester, NIACE.

Sutcliffe, J. and Simons, K. (1993). *Self-advocacy and Adults with Learning Difficulties*, Leicester, NIACE.

Torrance, H. and Pryor, J. (2001). 'How can classroom assessment be used to support children's learning?', *British Educational Research Journal*, Vol. 27, No.5, pp 615–31.

Vorhaus, J. (2000). 'Learning outcomes in a non-accredited curriculum: a view from the adult education sector', in Hayes, A., Lavender, P., Resisenberger, A. and Vorhaus, J., *Outcomes of Adult Learning*, Leicester, NIACE.

Weiner, B. (1984). 'Principles for a theory of motivation and their application within an attributional framework', in Ames, R and Ames, C., *Research on Motivation in Education*, Orlando, Academic Press.

Wertheimer, A. (ed) (1996). *Changing Days: Developing New Day Opportunities with People who have Learning Difficulties*, Kings Fund, London.

Related reading

Circle of Friends Movement (see **www.circlesnetwork.org.uk**).

Ecclestone, K. (1994). *Understanding Assessment: A Guide for Teachers and Managers in Post-compulsory Education*, Leicester, NIACE.

Mount, B. (2000). *Personal Futures Planning: Finding Directions for Change Using personal Futures Planning: A Sourcebook of values, Ideals and methods to Encourage person-centred development*, Capacity Works (available from Keepwell).

O'Brien, J. and Lovett, H. (1992). *Finding a way toward everyday lives: The contribution of person-centred planning*, Harrisburg Pennsylvania, Pennsylvania Office of Mental Retardation.

Ofsted (2002). *Inspecting Post-16 Provision for Learners with Learning Difficulties and/or Disabilities and for those with Special Educational Needs*.

People First **www.peoplefirst.org.uk**

Wolf, A. (1995). Competence-Based Assessment, Open University Press.